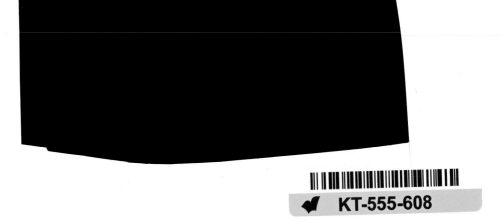

RAINY DAYS

SHADOW THEATRE

DENNY ROBSON
AND
VANESSA BAILEY

FRANKLIN WATTS
LONDON · NEW YORK · TORONTO · SYDNEY

CONTENTS

Design: David West
Children's Book Design
Photography: Roger Vlitos

© Aladdin Books Ltd 1990

Created and designed by
N.W. Books Ltd
28 Percy Street
London W1P 9FF

First published in
Great Britain in 1990 by
Franklin Watts Ltd
96 Leonard Street
London EC2A 4RH

ISBN 0-7496-0218-X

A CIP catalogue record for this book
is available from the British Library

Printed in Belgium

Introduction

Shadow theatre is one of the oldest forms of theatre in the world. India and China both have long traditions of shadow theatre. In Indonesia, the art of Wayang Purwa (*wayang* means shadow, *purwa* means ancient) grew out of primitive ancestor worship and is still performed today. Beautifully painted and gilded puppets of gods, demons and heroes cast shadows on a screen telling stories which teach people how to live wisely.

This book shows you how to become part of the world of shadow theatre. You can find out how to have fun creating hand shadows and how to put on a shadow play using jointed puppets. With a little imagination, some simple materials and a bit of practice, you can make shadows come alive!

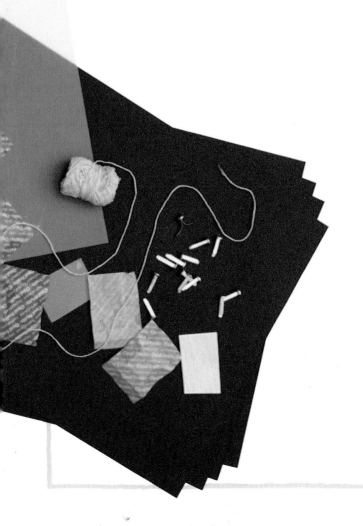

These are some of the materials we used to make the shadow puppets in this book. Once you have made the puppets, you may find you have lots of ideas for creating your own shadow characters.

Hand shadows

Hand shadows can be as simple or as complicated as you want to make them. The shadow creatures on the next few pages are quite easy to create, but with a little practice they can be made to act out dramas. Change the position of your fingers and they open and close their eyes. Experiment with different sound effects and move their mouths so that they appear to bark, neigh or screech. They can grow larger and smaller, chase each other or even fight to the death!

To create hand shadows you need a light source behind you and a plain wall in front. You could use a reading lamp, a torch or even sunlight. If you don't have a plain white wall, perhaps you could ask a grown-up to pin up a white sheet instead.

RABBIT

DOG

OSTRICH

Hand shadows

ELEPHANT

BIRD

PUNK ROCKER

BABY RABBIT

VULTURE

WOLF

7

Hand shadows with props

You can create a whole host of exciting hand shadows by using cut-out cardboard props. Quite simple shapes can prove very effective, like the rooster's comb below, or you can make more intricate cut-outs, like the group of knights doing battle on page 11. For these more complicated shadows, make sure you use a strong light source and have your hands quite close to the wall. That way the shadow will be as clear as possible and you will be able to see all the detail.

ROOSTER
This simple cardboard cut-out is the rooster's comb. Glue or tape a loop of card to its base for your finger. You can use your other hand to create the rooster's feathers.

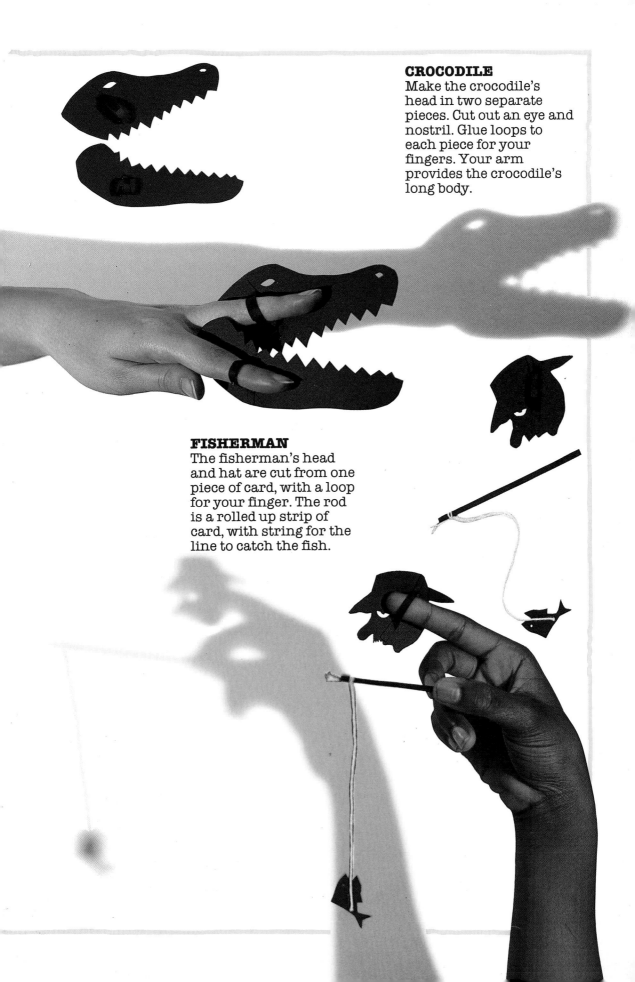

CROCODILE

Make the crocodile's head in two separate pieces. Cut out an eye and nostril. Glue loops to each piece for your fingers. Your arm provides the crocodile's long body.

FISHERMAN

The fisherman's head and hat are cut from one piece of card, with a loop for your finger. The rod is a rolled up strip of card, with string for the line to catch the fish.

Hand shadows with props

THE BOXERS
These mean-looking boxers are all ready to fight it out. Cut out their heads and boxing gloves and attach loops. Put them on your fingers as shown and let the match begin!

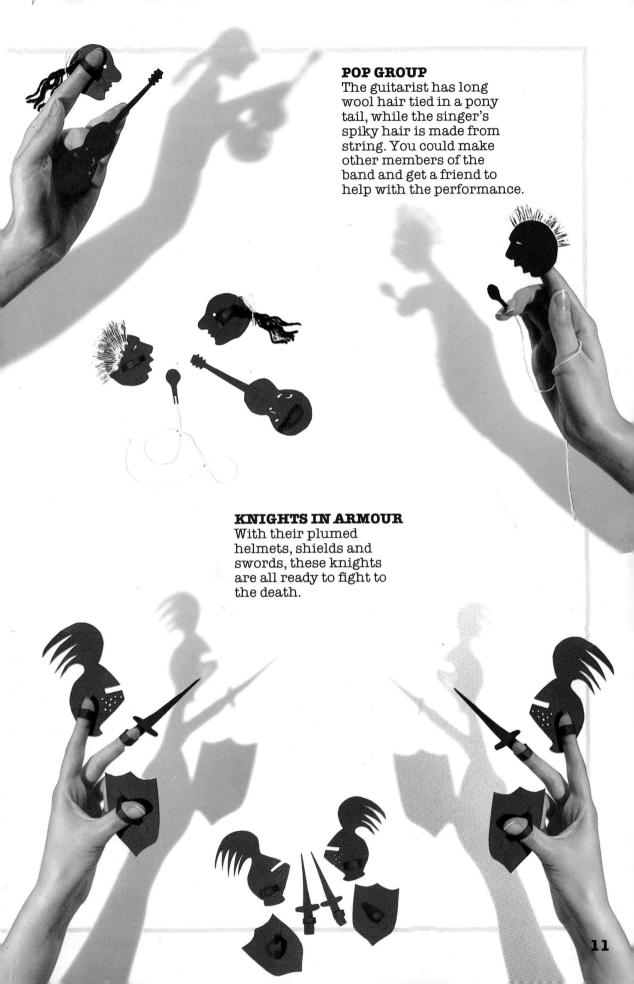

POP GROUP
The guitarist has long wool hair tied in a pony tail, while the singer's spiky hair is made from string. You could make other members of the band and get a friend to help with the performance.

KNIGHTS IN ARMOUR
With their plumed helmets, shields and swords, these knights are all ready to fight to the death.

Making a theatre

A shadow theatre has a translucent screen, which means it lets light shine through. Puppets perform behind the screen so that only the shadow of the figure is seen by the audience. You can make a shadow theatre in many different ways. It could be a picture frame with a piece of old sheet stretched across it or you could cut up a cardboard box, decorate it and tape tracing or greaseproof paper to it.

Our shadow theatre below is very simple to make. Cut a circle out of black card, colour some appropriate scenery onto tracing paper and glue this to the card. Tie or tape it to a chair and set up the light source.

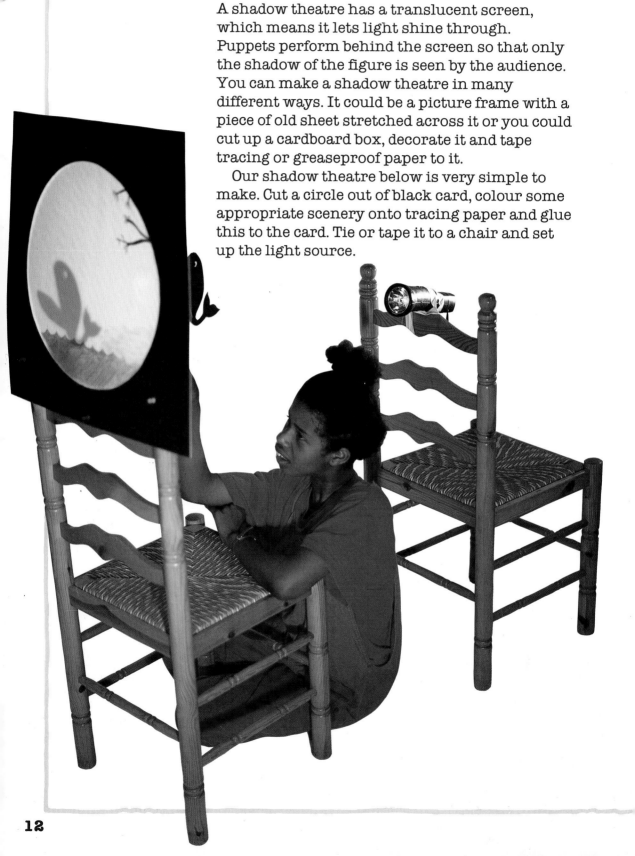

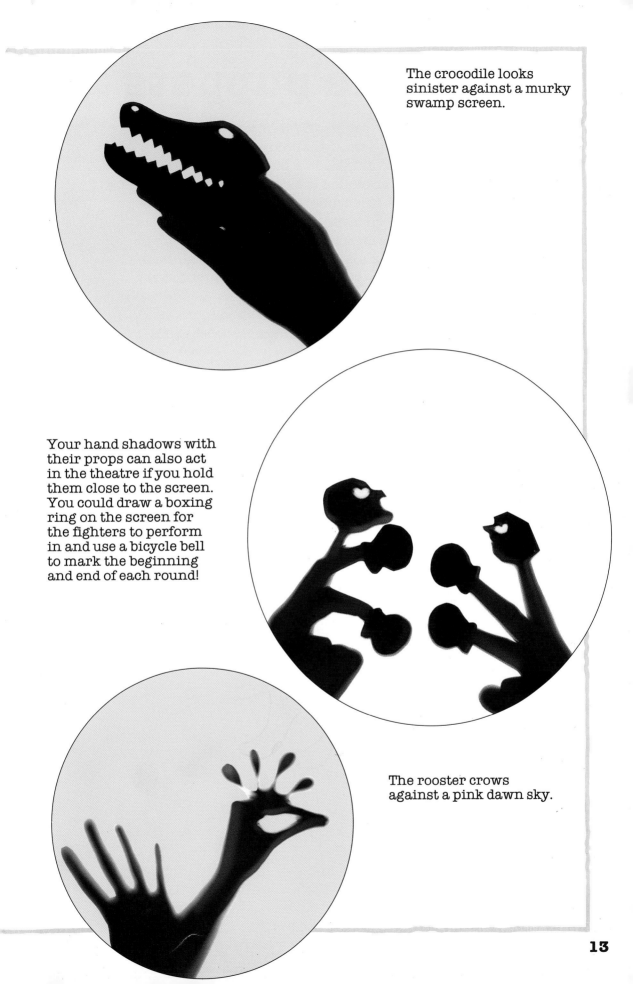

The crocodile looks sinister against a murky swamp screen.

Your hand shadows with their props can also act in the theatre if you hold them close to the screen. You could draw a boxing ring on the screen for the fighters to perform in and use a bicycle bell to mark the beginning and end of each round!

The rooster crows against a pink dawn sky.

Simple puppets

Shadow puppets are flat figures, worked by sticks or strings, that you hold against the screen. Traditional shadow puppets were made out of painted and oiled leather or parchment, but you can make excellent shadow puppets out of thin stiff cardboard.

It's a good idea to make lots of different puppets for your plays. The figures don't all have to look realistic — you can create scary monsters or creatures with one animal's head and another's body. Use your imagination to make them as funny, fierce, ridiculous or as beautiful as you like.

DINOSAUR
This rather fierce-looking stegosaurus is controlled by a stick glued to its back.

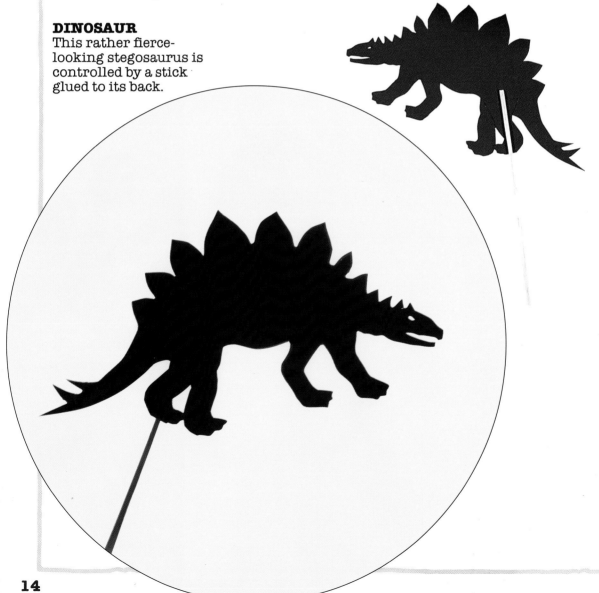

SPIDER
This big spooky spider with its sharp fangs showing is hanging by a thread behind the screen.

MONKEY
Paint your screen to look like a jungle and let the monkey swing through the trees by the thread tied to his tail.

Jointed puppets

Shadow puppets that appear to move parts of themselves can look very exciting. They can be simple, like the whale whose mouth opens and closes, or clever and complex, like our dancing clown on page 23. There are templates at the back of the book to help you make the more complicated puppets.

ORCHESTRA
You need two people to work this witty puppet, one to operate the conductor, and one the violinists. Join the conductor's arms to his body with a paper fastener. Make loops at either end of the row of violinists, slot in their bows and slide back and forth to make them play!

SONGBIRD
The bird is made in two parts and is jointed in such a way that its mouth opens and closes as it sings. Use the template if you need help.

WHALE
The whale's jaws are jointed and a thread is attached to the lower jaw. Pull on the thread and the whale opens and closes its mouth.

SKULL
The skull is made in two pieces, with a stick attached to the lower jaw and another to a framework on the upper jaw. Loosely tie the sticks together and move them up and down to make the skull speak!

Jointed puppets

SWINGING MONKEY
Cut out and assemble the monkey so that the limbs move freely. Thread string through the hands, hold each end and the monkey will swing.

MISS MUFFET
Shake the stick supporting Miss Muffet to make her legs and skirt move. Pull on the strings attached to the tops of her arms and her hands go up and down.

LION AND LION-TAMER

Use the templates to draw the shapes, cut them out and assemble using paper fasteners. Thread a piece of cotton through the lion's jaw as shown. Pull and release to make the lion close and open his mouth.

The lion-tamer's whip is a piece of string. Tie thread to the tops of his arms and jerk the cotton to make him lash out with his whip.

Coloured puppets

Not all shadow puppets cast black shadows. They can also be brightly and beautifully coloured. You have already seen that you can create faces on black card puppets by cutting out shapes so that the light shines through. By gluing coloured cellophane (sweet wrappers are a good source), coloured film or tissue across these cut-outs, your puppet can seem more alive. Monsters can have red glinting eyes, king's wear jewelled crowns and dragons become more fantastic.

GARDEN SCENE

The bright colours of the flower are pieces of cellophane which have been glued to the black card cut-out. The butterfly has been made with card and clear acetate film coloured with felt pens.

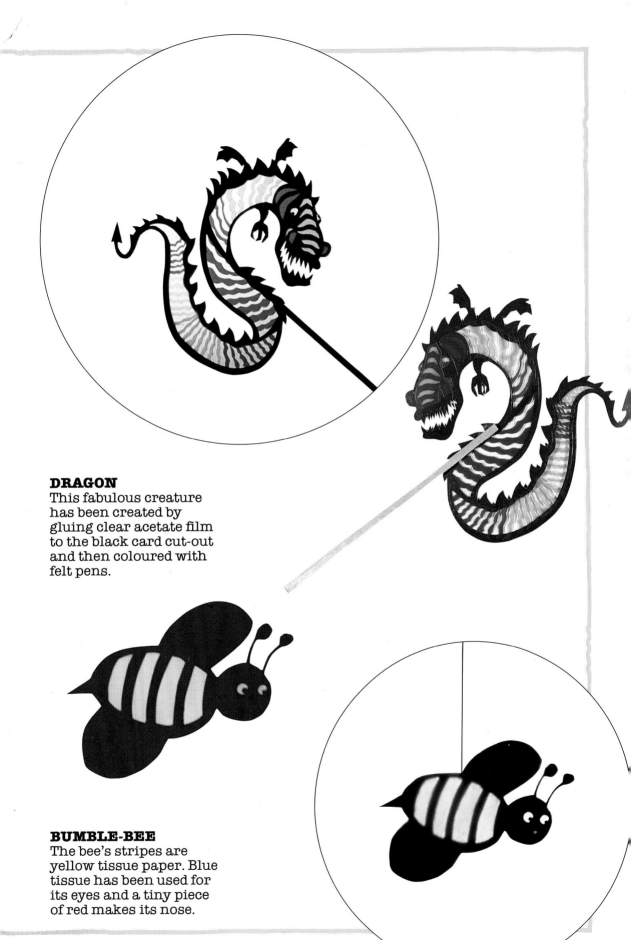

DRAGON

This fabulous creature
has been created by
gluing clear acetate film
to the black card cut-out
and then coloured with
felt pens.

BUMBLE-BEE

The bee's stripes are
yellow tissue paper. Blue
tissue has been used for
its eyes and a tiny piece
of red makes its nose.

Jointed coloured puppets

Once you have made some shadow puppets, starting with the simple one-piece shapes and experimenting with puppets with moving parts, you are ready to try the more complex coloured puppets. Then perhaps you can use these basic techniques to create a whole range of characters of your own.

JEWELLED FISH
This beautiful creature is made in the same way as the whale (page 17), except that sections have been cut out and coloured film inserted to make it look more exotic.

DANCING CLOWN

Tie the legs together, the arms together and then link them with another piece of string. When you pull on the string, the clown will dance!

SNAKE

The snake is made in separate sections, with each piece tied to the next. You can make it as long as you want, although you may need more sticks to support it.

The play

You have made your theatre, the puppets are ready and now it's time to make the shadows come alive. First you have to decide on your story. Simple stories are easiest for your audience to follow. Work out which puppets will be used and how many helpers you will need. It might even be a good idea to write out a script. Colour up the scenery and don't forget to rehearse any sound effects — they can really make the play come to life.

In the fisherman's play, we use a hand shadow as well as shadow puppets.

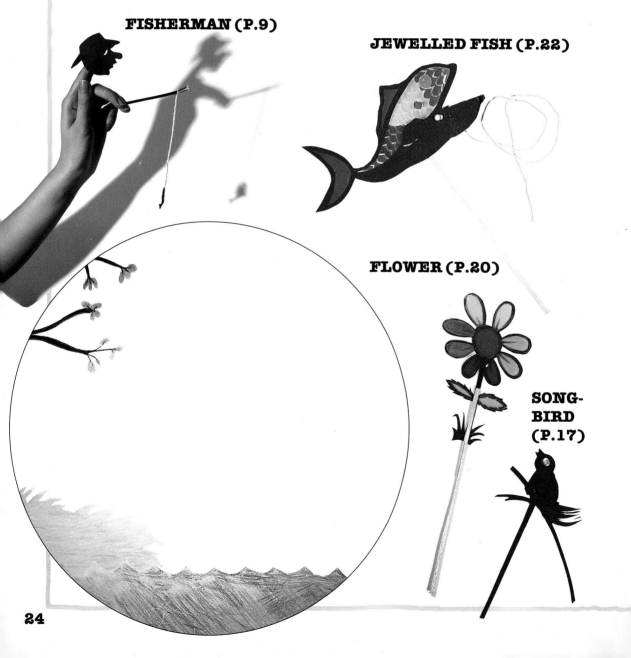

FISHERMAN (P.9)

JEWELLED FISH (P.22)

FLOWER (P.20)

SONG-BIRD (P.17)

The birds are singing, the flowers are blooming, but the fisherman is not having much luck on the riverbank.

Suddenly the rod is almost jerked from his hand. He is sure it must be an enormous fish. He draws out a tiddler.

The fisherman sighs and throws the fish back. From the depths of the river, a huge jewelled fish appears.

Its mighty jaws clamp over the fish and it dives back down to the depths .... pulling the poor fisherman with it!

Tales and nursery rhymes

There really is no limit to the stories you can act out in shadow theatre. Your characters can be anything you want them to be and they can do anything you want them to do. Transformation stories — where one creature turns into another — work very well in shadow theatre because the audience doesn't see you making the change. But if you don't want to make up your own play, there are lots of fairytales and nursery rhymes you could choose from.

In this play we act out the nursery rhyme of Little Miss Muffet, using a jointed shadow puppet and the more simple spider. Remember to draw your scenery to suit your play.

MISS MUFFET (P.18)

SPIDER (P.15)

26

Little Miss Muffet
Sat on a tuffet,

Eating her curds and whey;

There came a big spider,

Who sat down beside her....
And frightened Miss Muffet away!

Template help

Trace these shapes on to card and cut out to make the more complicated shadow puppets.

ORCHESTRA (A,B,C,D)

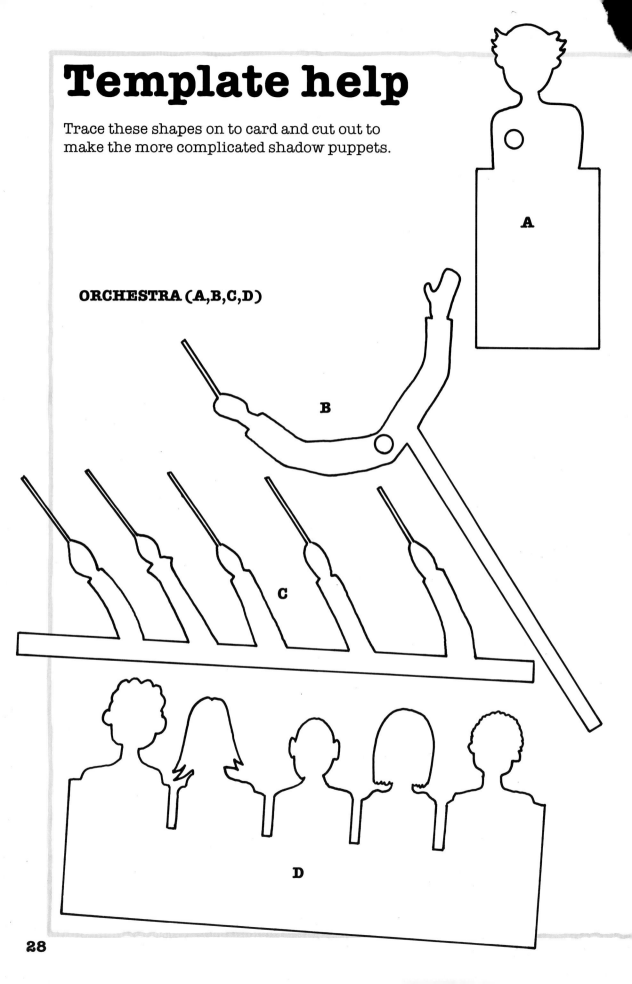

A

B

C

D

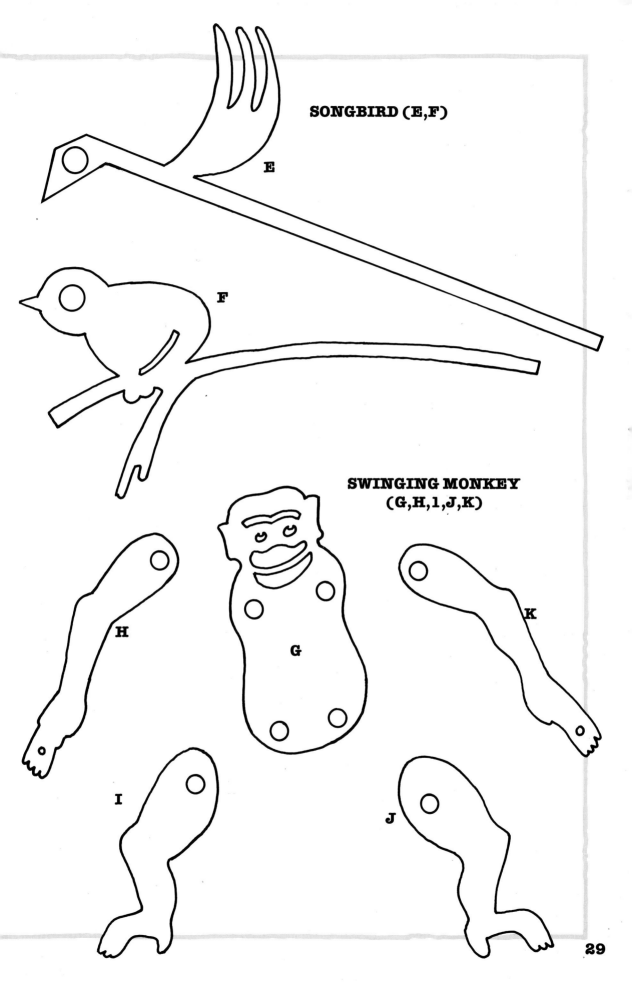

SONGBIRD (E,F)

E

F

SWINGING MONKEY
(G,H,1,J,K)

H

K

G

I

J

29

Template help

MISS MUFFET (A,B,C,D,E,F)

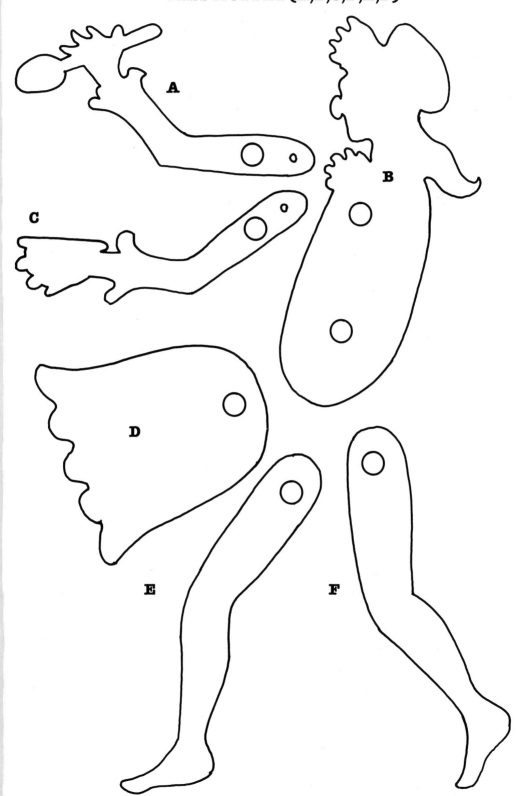

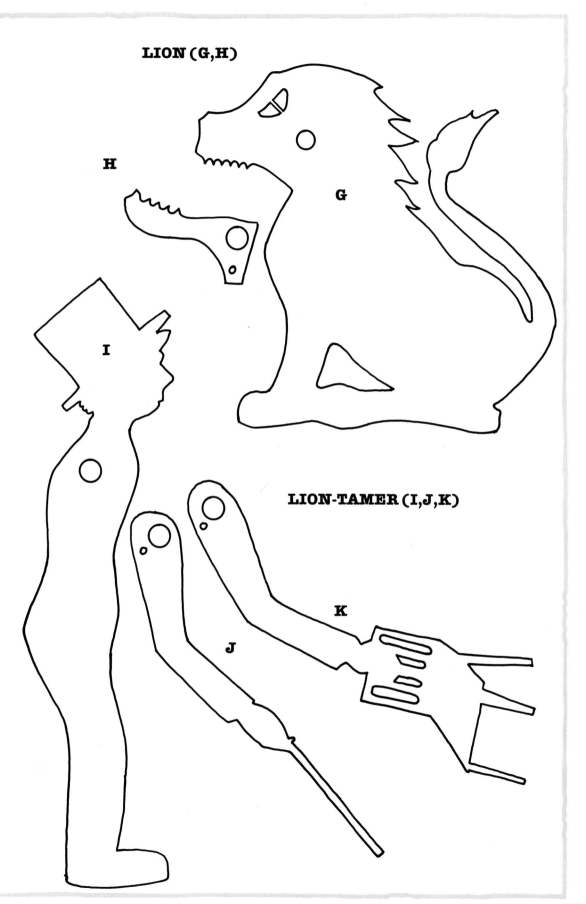

LION (G,H)

H

G

I

LION-TAMER (I,J,K)

K

J

Template help

DANCING CLOWN (A,B,C,D,E)

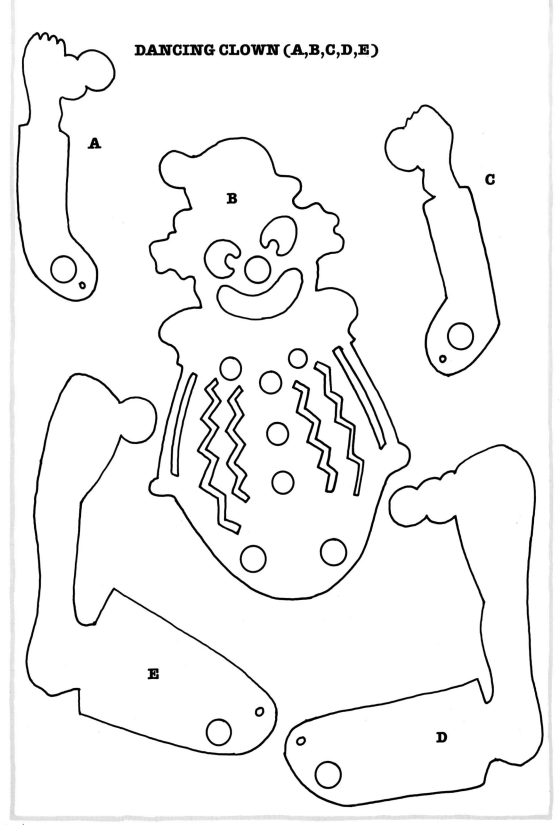

PRINTED IN BELGIUM BY
proost
INTERNATIONAL BOOK PRODUCTION